THE M

OF 52

written by Emily Climer
illustrated by Madelyn Goodnight

Page ii, Lynne Munson; page iii, Ralph White/Getty Images; page 4, Blue Planet Archive/Alamy Stock Photo; pages 20-21, 31 (bottom), Nature Picture Library/Alamy Stock Photo; pages 26-27, 31 (center left), 41 (top and bottom), 53 (bottom) WaterFrame/Alamy Stock Photo; page 30, page 53 (center), by wildestanimal/Moment/Getty Images; page 31 (top), M.M. Sweet/Moment/Getty Images; pages 34-35 (top), Image Source Limited/Alamy Stock Photo, (bottom), Science Photo Library/Science Source; pages 44-45, Karen Debler/Alamy Stock Photo; pages 48-49, Claude Huot/Alamy Stock Photo; pages 50-51, Reinhard Dirscherl/Alamy Stock Photo; page 53 (top), Masa Ushioda/Alamy Stock Photo; More page, Avalon.red /Alamy Stock Photo.

All other images are the property of Great Minds.

CONTENTS

CHAPTER 1:
A SEA OF SOUNDS

Clicks and pulses. Deep rumbles. Long, low moans. In the darkness of the deep sea, sound can tell us many things.

The ocean covers most of our planet, but its depth makes it hard to study. Most of the ocean is so deep that light cannot reach the bottom. But sound can travel to places where sunlight cannot go.

The sea has a world of sounds. Ships, oil drills, fish, and other sea life all make sounds in the water. So do storms and earthquakes. To better study the ocean, experts have invented ways to track its sounds.

One way people track the sounds is by using hydrophones, or underwater microphones. The U.S. Navy has used hydrophones for decades to track enemy submarines. In 1989, the navy's hydrophones picked up a mysterious sound in the ocean off the West Coast of the United States. It was a low moan.

This hydrophone picks up sound waves as they move through the water and then sends the sound data up to the ship. Researchers record the sound data on a computer for further study.

The people who heard the low moan were puzzled. They had never heard a sound like this before. At first, it sounded like a machine. They thought it might even be an enemy submarine, but they weren't sure. Because their work was secret, the Navy could not share the sound for several years. When they did, they knew just who to ask for help.

CHAPTER 2:
AN EXPERT ON SEA SOUNDS

Bill Watkins was just the person for the job.

He had lived a life that taught him how to listen.

As a child, Bill loved to listen to people speak. Bill's parents were from the United States, but they raised him in West Africa. Growing up in West Africa, Bill heard three primary languages: English, French, and Fula. Over time, he learned to speak all three and many more.

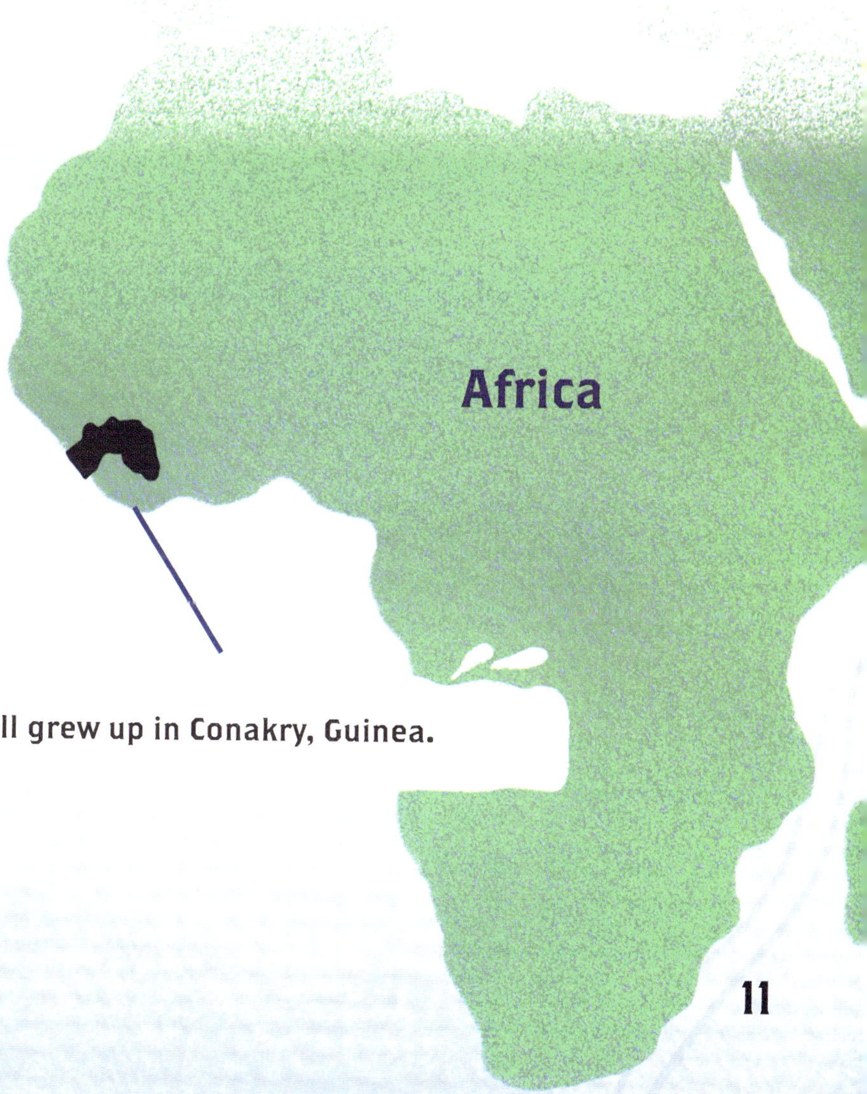

Bill grew up in Conakry, Guinea.

As Bill got older, he kept listening. In college, he learned how sound travels and how to record sounds. He went on to build his own radio station in West Africa.

In 1957, Bill moved back to the U.S. He got a job that would use his recording skills in a brand-new way. Bill would no longer record people. Instead, he would record animals—animals at sea.

The place where Bill worked had a big problem. They wanted to be able to record sounds at sea, but their equipment kept breaking in rough waters. Bill invented new equipment that could survive the wind and waves. Now, scientists could travel closer to sea animals and record their sounds.

Bill Watkins (right) worked for the Woods Hole Oceanographic Institution. Together, he and scientist William Schevill (left) invented new tools for tracking underwater sounds.

Bill loved recording the sounds of sea animals. He felt it was one of the best ways to learn about them. Over the years, Bill collected and sorted recordings of hundreds of sea animals. By the time the navy came calling, he had become an expert on whales and their calls.

When the navy shared the strange sound, Bill could not believe what he heard. This did not sound like any whale call he knew. And yet, it had the features of a whale call. It was pitched very low. It would repeat. And it would move from spot to spot, just like a migrating whale.

"Could this be a blue whale?" Bill thought. But the pitch of the sound was very strange.

People measure how high or low the pitch of a sound is by using hertz. A high hertz number means a high pitch. This whale call was 52 hertz.

52 hertz is a very low-pitched sound for a person, like a low note on a tuba. But for a blue whale, 52 hertz is very high-pitched. Most blue whales have a call that is pitched at 15 to 20 hertz, which is beyond human hearing. Bill had never heard a blue whale call so high.

People gave the whale a nickname: 52. Bill didn't know it, but he was about to follow 52 for a very long time.

Sound travels in waves. Frequency measures how fast a wave vibrates. High-pitched sounds make waves that vibrate rapidly and that look close together on paper. Low-pitched sounds make waves that vibrate more slowly and look far apart.

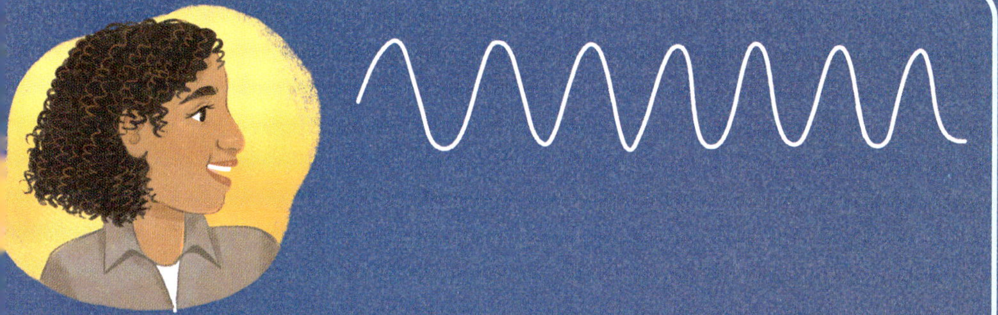

Human Voice – – 100–250 hertz

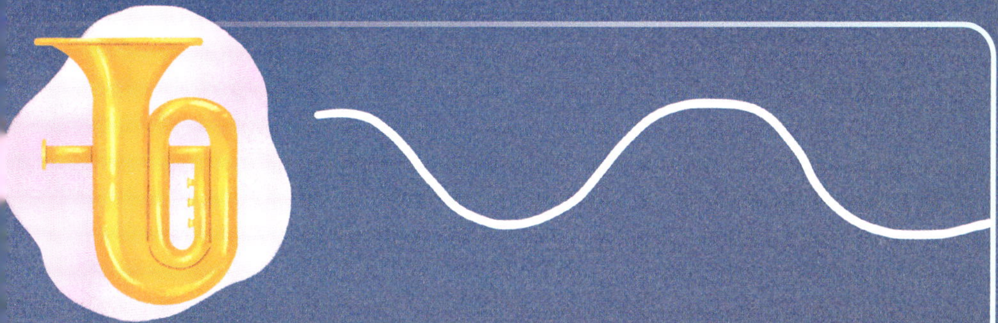

Tuba – – – – – – – 30–60 hertz

Blue Whale – – – – – 15–20 hertz

CHAPTER 3:
THE MYSTERY OF 52

The first step to solving a mystery is asking good questions. Bill and his team had many questions about 52:

Was the same whale making the call every time?
Could any other whales hear the call?

In search of answers, Bill set out to track 52. But tracking a sound is hard in the vast darkness of the ocean.

Close your eyes and listen to the sounds in the room. Can you tell exactly where they are coming from without looking? Now, imagine you are in a space that is many miles wide. You hear noises far away. Can you tell where the sounds are coming from now? In the same way, it was hard for Bill and his team to know where 52 was in the deep, dark sea.

In fact, before 52, scientists had only been able to track any whale for a few hours, maybe a day at the most. Luckily, 52's call was so unique that Bill and his team could track the whale for much longer.

Of course, tracking a whale's call doesn't mean that you can find the whale's exact location. It takes time for the sound data to travel to the nearest hydrophone. By the time the scientists hear the call, the whale has likely moved.

If Bill and his team had been able to see 52, they probably could have figured out what kind of whale it was. Bill knew three species of whales traveled in the same waters as 52: blue, fin, and humpback.

BLUE
FIN
HUMPBACK

These three species look very different. Blue whales have grown up to 110 feet long, making them the biggest animals on planet Earth. Fin whales have tall, curved dorsal fins on their backs. And as their name suggests, humback whales have a small hump in front of their dorsal fins.

Whale tails, called flukes, often have scars or markings. Humpback flukes have particularly distinct black-and-white markings that can be used to tell individual whales apart.

As hard as the team tried, they could not catch a glimpse of 52. Not a fin, not a fluke, not even a spout of water.

To solve the mystery of 52, they would have to rely on its call.

CHAPTER 4:

WHALES AND THEIR CALLS

Some whales make clicking sounds to figure out where they are in the ocean. Some whales whistle to talk to each other or use pulses to hunt their prey. And some, including blue whales, even sing songs in the deep.

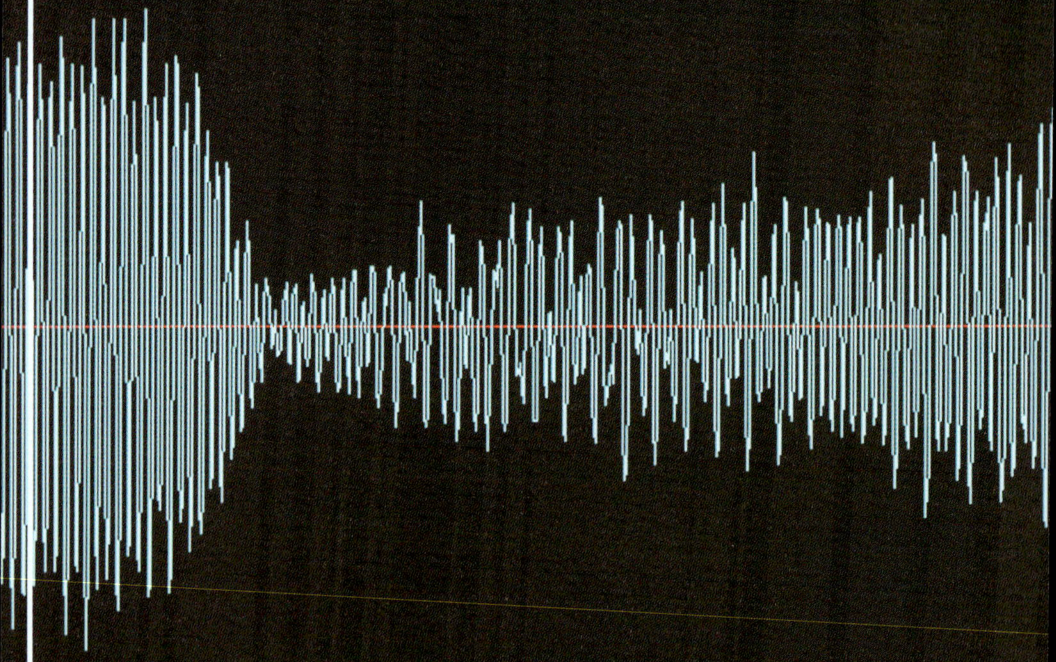

These soundwaves were made by a humpback whale. Humpback songs range from 20 to 24,000 hertz.

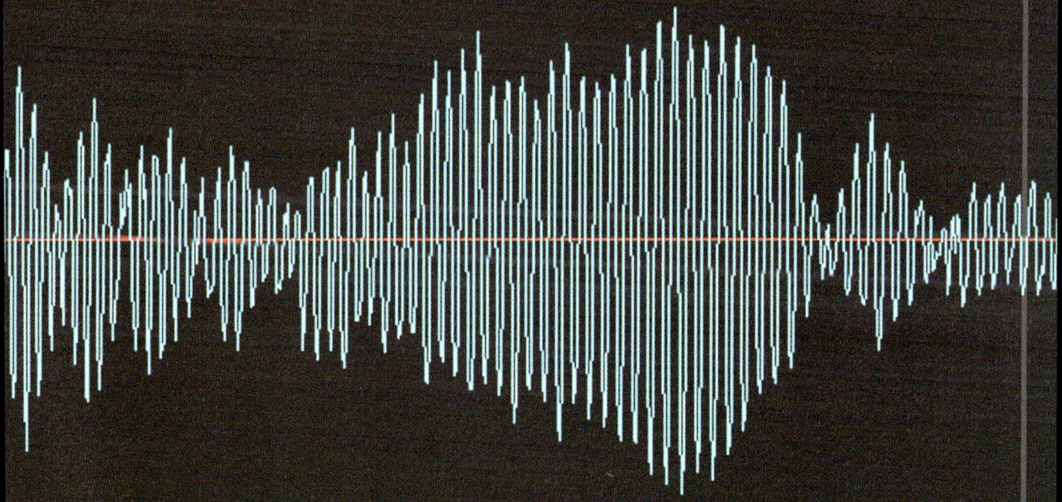

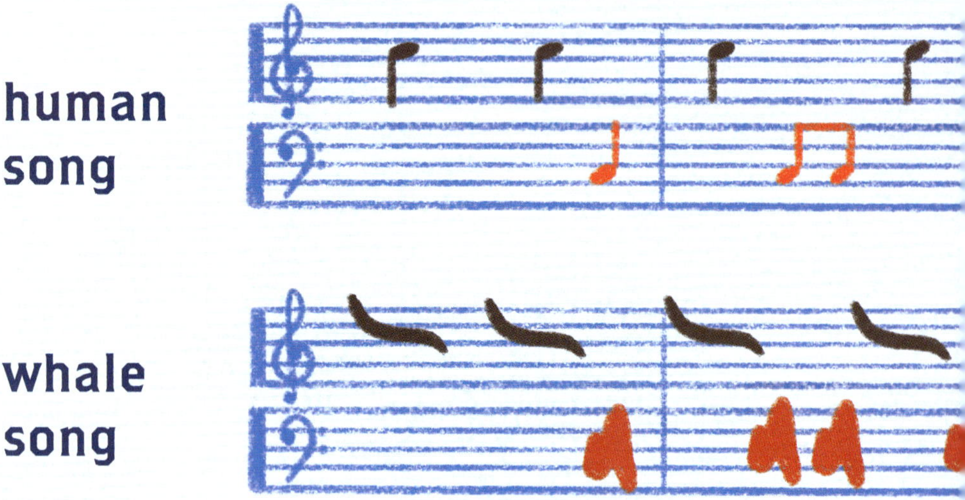

A whale song, like a human song, is made of patterns of sound. Hum a song in your head. To do this, first you string together notes to make a phrase of music. Then, you repeat phrases to make a verse. Finally, you combine a few verses to sing a song. Whale songs have these patterns, too. A whale links short units of sound to make a phrase. Then it combines a few phrases into a theme. A few themes make up a song.

Bill spent his life learning about the sounds and songs of different whale species. He listened to thousands of hours of recordings. He used this knowledge as he tracked 52.

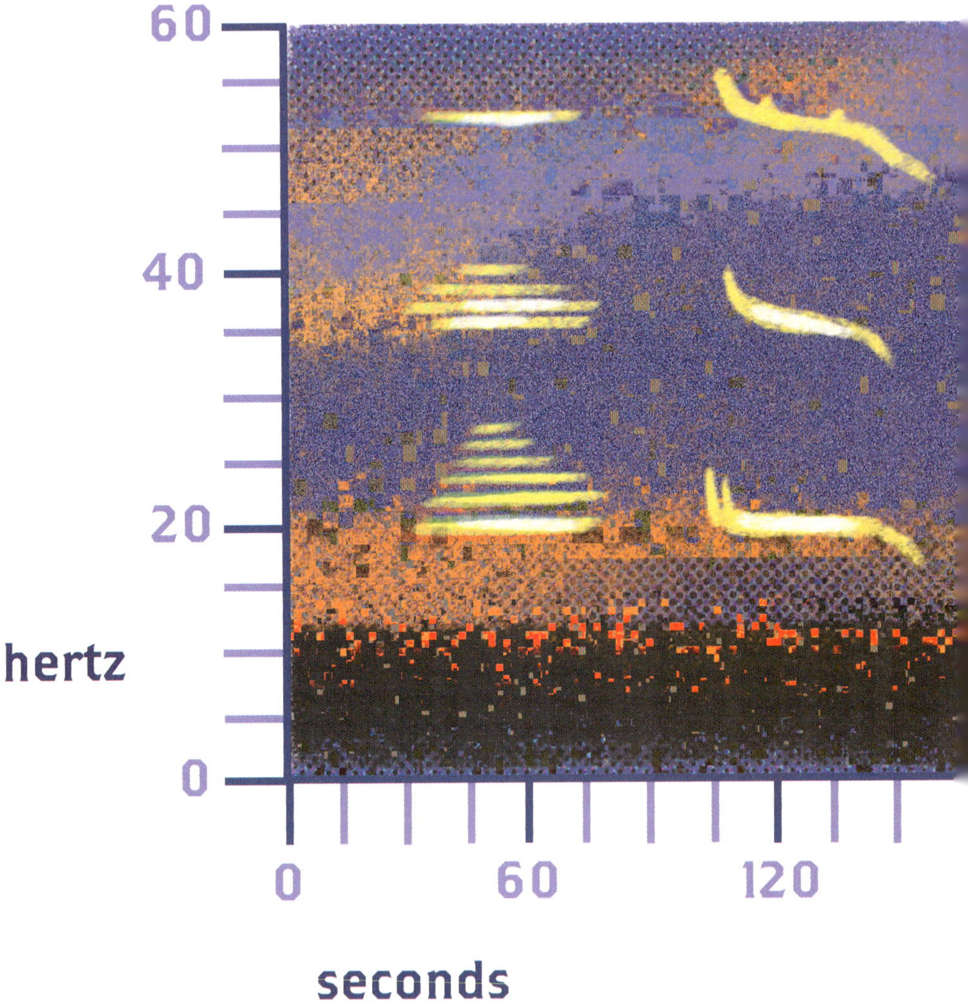

A spectrogram is a visual way to show sounds. The vertical scale on the left side shows the pitch of the sound. The horizontal scale at the bottom shows the time. The darkness of the image depicts variations in volume. Spectrograms help experts study whale songs in depth.

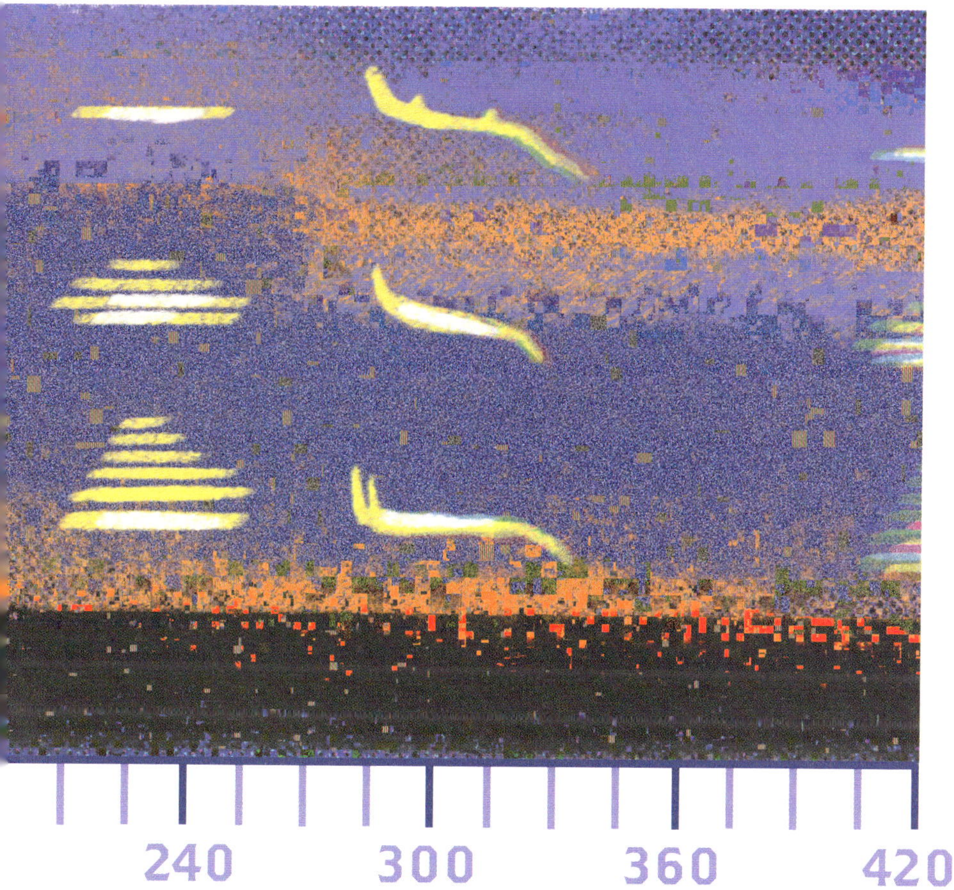

THE DEEP TONES OF BLUE WHALES

For blue whales, a big body means big sounds. Blue whales are some of the loudest animals in the world. One blue whale's song can be as loud as a jet plane. In fact, a blue whale can be heard up to hundreds of miles away. That is like shouting in New York and someone hearing you in Florida!

New York
Florida

Even though they are loud, blue whale calls are pitched so low that people often can't hear their deep tones. When Bill recorded blue whales, he had to speed up the recording so that the pitch would be high enough to hear.

Today, experts think that blue whale songs may be getting lower pitched over time. When they listen to recordings from the past, they hear whales singing in a higher pitch.

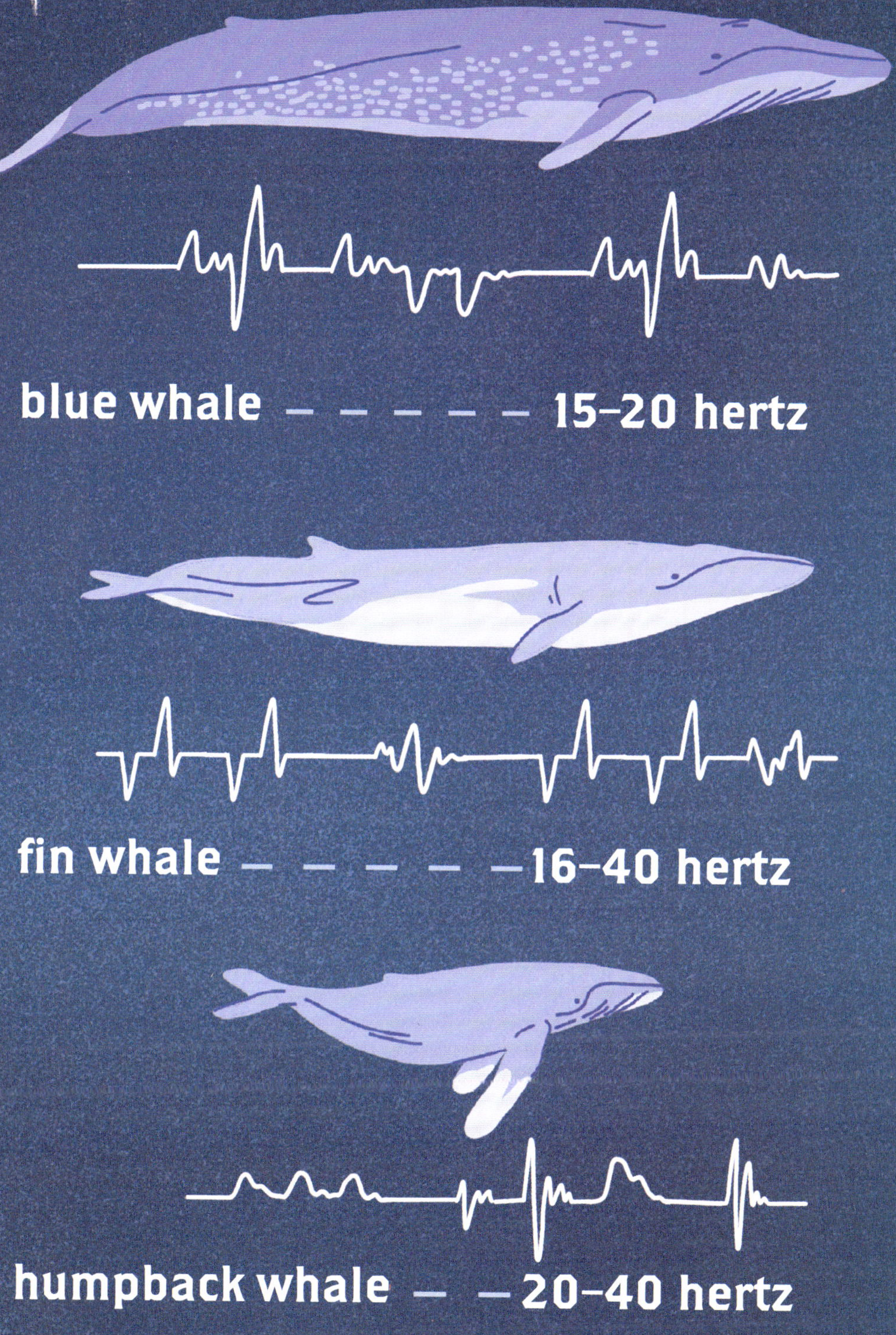
blue whale – – – – – 15–20 hertz
fin whale – – – – – –16–40 hertz
humpback whale – –20–40 hertz

THE SHORT PULSES OF FIN WHALES

As the second-largest whales, fin whales also make very loud calls. These whales also sing some of the simplest songs. Fin whale songs are made up of short calls, or pulses, that repeat every 7 to 40 seconds or so.

Each pulse is about 20 hertz. So when a fin whale sings, it repeats the same note over and over again.

Bill first started recording the calls of fin whales in 1958. For the most part, he heard 20-hertz pulses. But every so often, he heard a much higher pitch. Bill recorded fin whale pulses as high as 75 hertz, which is an even higher-pitched sound than 52's call. These high notes would only happen when other fin whales were close by.

Fin whale songs are so loud that the sound waves can pass through rock in the ocean floor. Some researchers in 2021 hoped to use fin whale songs to learn about the thickness of the ocean floor.

THE COMPLEX PATTERNS OF HUMPBACK WHALES

Male humpback whales sing the most complex songs in the sea. One humpback song may have many patterns of sound. Humpback whales even change their songs over time. When singing, a whale may add a phrase, change a phrase, or even cut one out.

Other whales may copy the song and pass it along in their pod. Within a year or two, whales up and down the coast may be singing the same new song.

When Bill recorded humpback whales, they often sang in groups—and their songs could last several hours. The humpback songs seemed connected to their migration from one spot in the sea to the next.

Today, researchers have observed humpback whales passing their songs from one population to another as the whales travel across the Pacific Ocean. A song can travel thousands of miles in just a couple years.

Bill knew the deep tones of blue whales, the short pulses of fin whales, and the complex songs of humpback whales. But did 52 sound like any of these whales? Not quite. While 52's call shared features in common with these whales, it was truly unlike any other call Bill had heard.

Chapter 5:
A Call Unlike Any Other

"It is unusual to recognize the call of an individual whale more than a few hours," Bill wrote in 2004. At the time, his team had been tracking 52 for 12 years! Bill was used to following groups of whales together, not one whale at a time. 52's high pitch, sudden stops and starts, and repeating sounds meant that the team could tell 52 apart from other whales. The team could track the call without losing it in all the other songs and sounds of the sea. But the same things that made 52's call easier to track also made it a mystery.

Blue, fin, and humpback whales live for about 80 to 90 years, but some have lived up to 111 years!

humpback whale

fin whale

blue whale

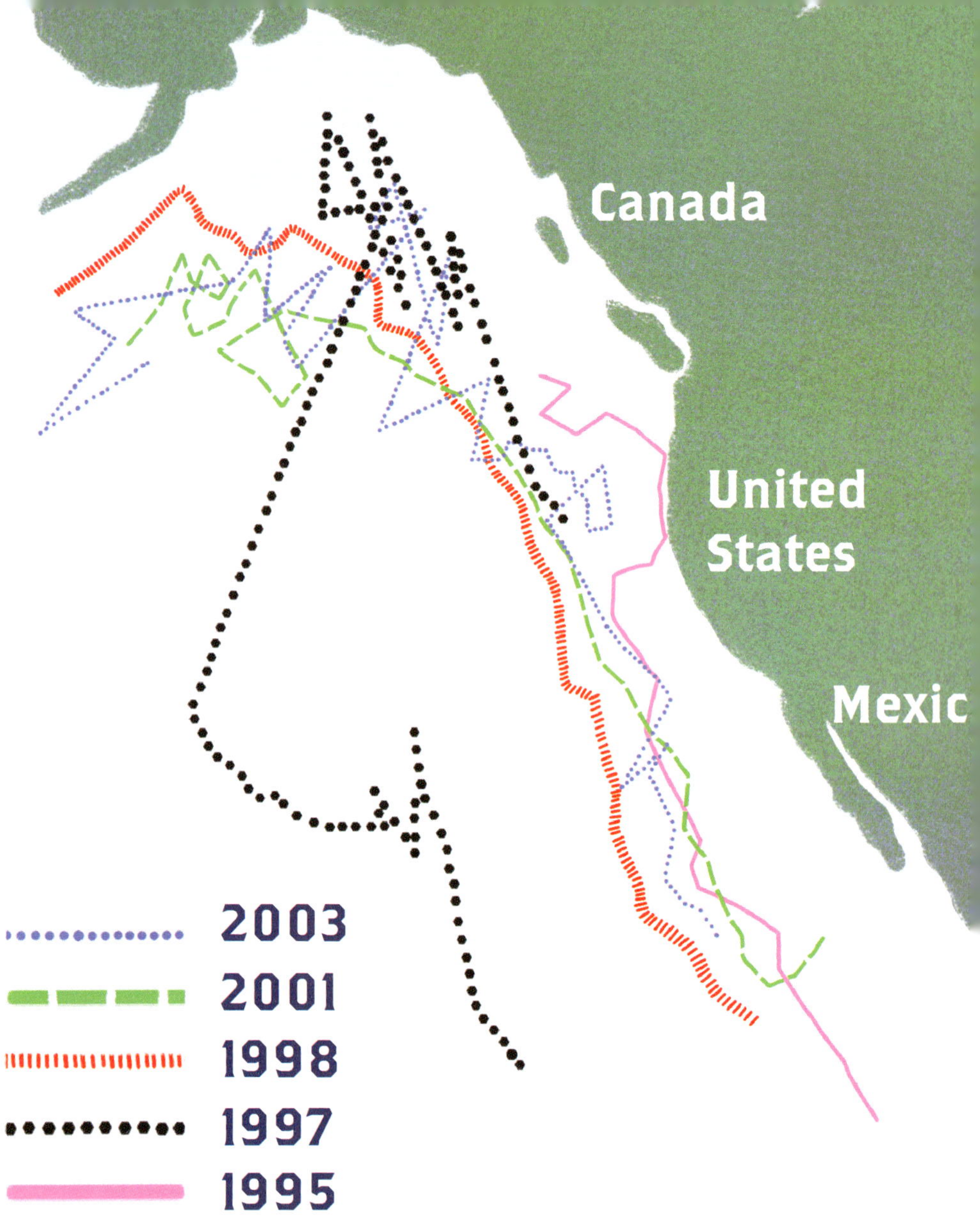

The colored paths above show 52's travels each year.

As the team tracked 52 over the years, they made maps of its path each year. They also tracked pods of whales. The team would try to match 52's path with the path of a blue, fin, or humpback whale pod. They thought that if 52 traveled with other whales, it might belong to their pod. Then the team could listen to the other calls from 52's pod and make a good guess about what kind of whale it was.

But 52's path did not overlap with any other paths the team had tracked. As difficult as it was to believe, these strange calls seemed to come from just one whale. And as far as they could tell at that time, 52 was traveling alone.

Bill *still* didn't have the answer to his question about what kind of whale 52 might be. But he did have new ideas. What if 52 wasn't just one species of whale? Could it be a cross between two kinds of whales? If that was true, 52 would be a hybrid whale.

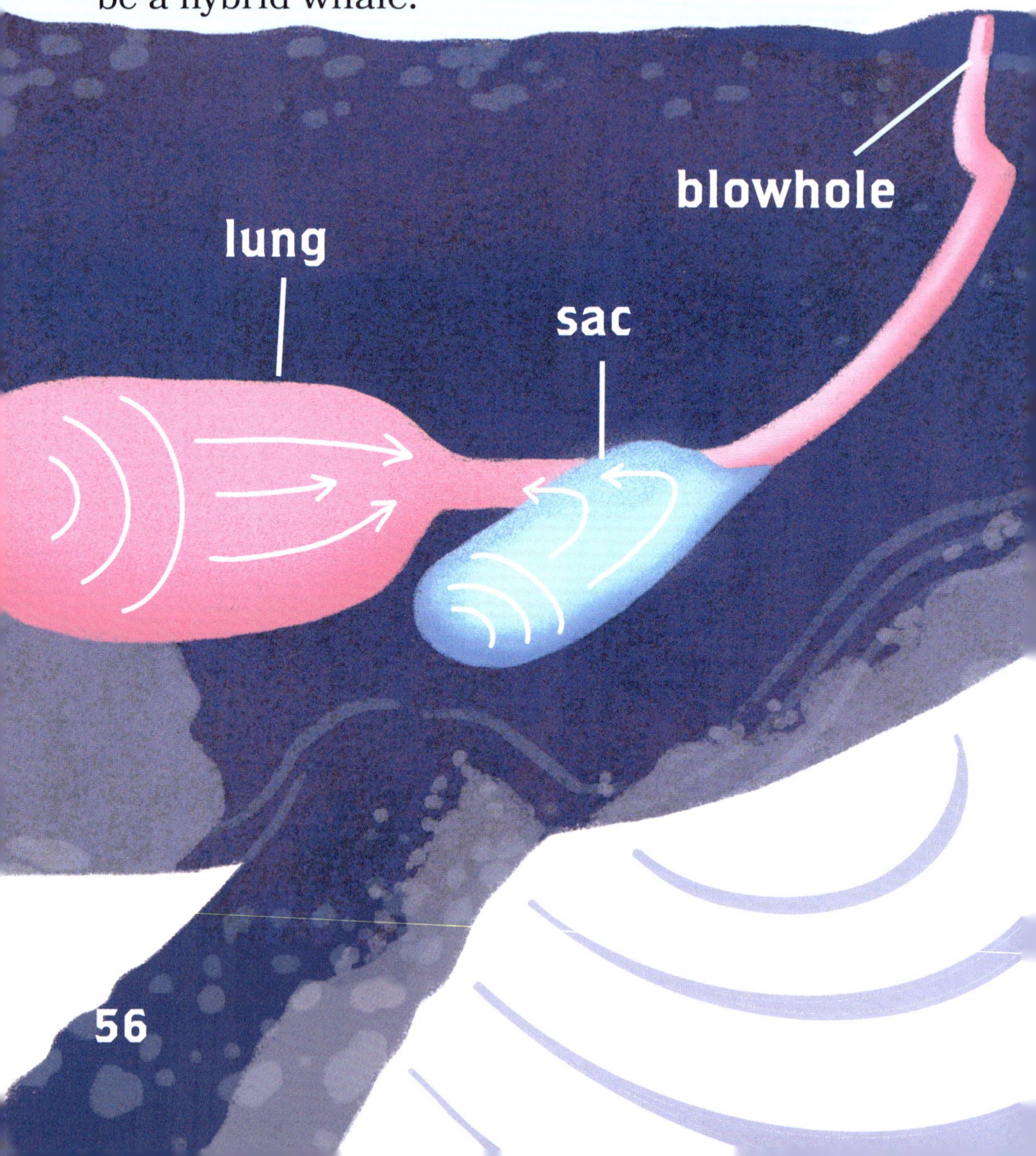

There was also another possibility: 52's sound organs may have formed differently than in other whales of its kind. This, too, could explain why 52 made a call so unlike any other.

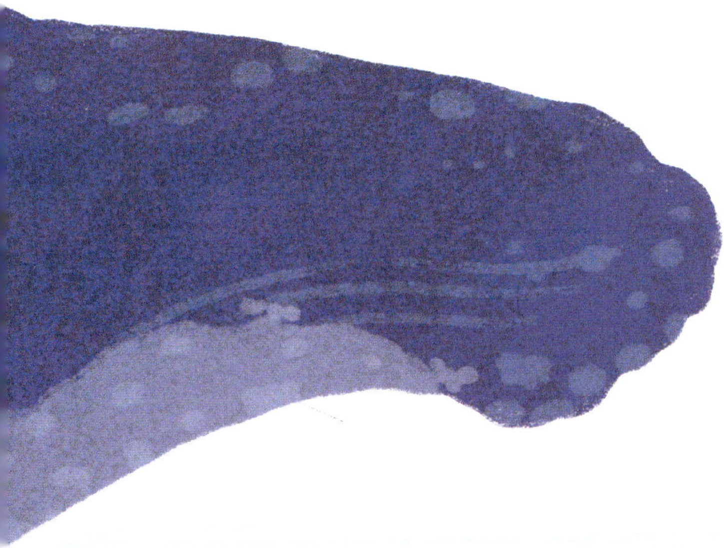

Unlike humans, whales don't exhale when they sing. Scientists think that air passes back and forth between the whale's lungs and its sacs that store air. As air passes into the sacs, it crosses folds of skin. The folds vibrate, which makes sound. The sound is so loud that it can travel from inside the whale through many miles of water.

Bill was never able to solve the mystery of 52. But he left behind something just as important: a database of sounds. When he died in 2004, Bill had added over 20,000 calls from more than 60 species of sea creatures. Many are whale songs.

More than anything else, Bill Watkins felt it was important to share the sounds of the sea. He knew just how much we had to learn from listening. And because of Bill, people still search for 52 to this day.

We wonder if we'll ever get to see the whale with such a strange call. And mostly, we wonder *What will we learn when we do?*

"What we can hear in the ocean is much more powerful than what we can see." –Bill Watkins

MORE

To learn about whales, Bill Watkins and his team first had to find them. Whales are very large animals, but they can be tricky to find in vast, dark oceans.

Bill and his team developed a radio tag to track the location of whales. It took years! The radio tag included batteries and a long antenna. The tag attached to a thick layer of skin and fat, called blubber, on the whale. When the whale surfaced, the tag reported the whale's location by sending a radio signal. The signal traveled from the antenna to tracking equipment on a ship. This helped Bill identify and locate certain whales.

Today, scientists use satellite tags to track whales. These tags track whales by sending signals to satellites orbiting high above Earth. Satellite tags give information about the whales' movements, like how deep they dive underwater. Some tags can even record sounds or video. Researchers also use drones, cameras, and other technology to monitor whales. All these tools help scientists learn more about how whales travel and move in the ocean.